South Beach Diet Desserts: Delicious Desserts That Promote Weight Loss and Allow You To Stick To Your Diet

All rights Reserved. No part of this publication or the information in it may be quoted from or reproduced in any form by means such as printing, scanning, photocopying or otherwise without prior written permission of the copyright holder.

Disclaimer and Terms of Use: Effort has been made to ensure that the information in this book is accurate and complete, however, the author and the publisher do not warrant the accuracy of the information, text and graphics contained within the book due to the rapidly changing nature of science, research, known and unknown facts and internet. The Author and the publisher do not hold any responsibility for errors, omissions or contrary interpretation of the subject matter herein. This book is presented solely for motivational and informational purposes only.

Table of Contents

Phase Two Desserts 5

   Berry Parfait 6

   Ricotta Cheesecake 7

   Chocolate covered apricots 8

   Cherry Cheese pie 9

   Fudgecicle 10

   Explosive Cheesecake 11

   Key Lime pie 12

   Crème 13

   Chopped Strawberries 14

   Cinnamon Crème 15

   Winter Snow pudding 16

   Spice Cookies 17

   Apple Almonds 18

   Chocolate cookies 19

   Peanut butter drops 20

   PB&J Cookie 21

   Decadent chocolate pudding 22

   Custard 23

   Chocolate pecan pie 24

   Peanut Butter Cups 25

   Frozen Frosting 26

   Brownie Balls 27

   Peanut butter fruit dip 28

   Chai Pudding 29

   Mini cheesecakes 30

Apple Crisp 31

South Beach Bars 32

Pink Pie 33

Sour Cream cheesecake 34

Sugar Free layered cream cheese 35

Phase Two Desserts

Berry Parfait

Ingredients:
- 3 Large strawberries
- ¼ C fresh blueberries (or thawed)
- ¾ C sugar free vanilla pudding
- ¼ C granola cereal
- 1 T sugar free cool whip

Directions: this is really simple, start layering everything with the strawberries on the bottom, then part of the pudding, then cereal, followed by blueberries, than pudding again and so on, until you run out, the last thing (or on the top) should be the cool whip

Ricotta Cheesecake

Ingredients:
- 2 C ricotta
- 3 T Splenda
- 1 tsp vanilla extract
- ½ C vanilla bean (scraped)
- 2 eggs

Directions:

1. Mix everything together well, and scoop into ramekins and bake at 350 for roughly 20-25 minutes.

Chocolate covered apricots

Ingredients:
- 2 oz. bittersweet chocolate chips
- 2 dozen dried apricots
- 1 T chopped almonds

Directions:

1. You need to melt down the chocolate chips either in a saucepan without letting the chocolate stick to the pan or burn, or in the microwave. Either way you can't let it burn.
2. Dip the apricots in the smooth melted chocolate.
3. Then set the apricots on wax paper and sprinkle the crushed almonds over the apricots.

Cherry Cheese pie

Ingredients:
- 2 8 oz. packages of fat free cream cheese
- 2 T fat free ricotta
- 2 T sugar free syrup
- 2 T cherry sugar free syrup
- ½ C Splenda
- 1 packet original flavor (or unflavored) gelatin
- 1 C boiling water

Direction:

1. Soften the cream cheese and ricotta together mix well with hand mixer or blender.
2. Once this is done you can set it aside.
3. In a separate bowl add your syrups, gelatin and Splenda and 1 C boiling hot water stirring until gelatin dissolves.
4. Now you can add your two bowls so mixes now and beat with mixer until very smooth no lumps at all.
5. Pour these into muffin tins or in cupcake covers. Let this sit in fridge overnight.
6. Generally good after about 2 hours.

Fudgecicle

Ingredients:
- 1 ¼ C skim milk
- 1 T cocoa powder
- 3 T Splenda

Directions:

1. Mix everything until smooth and pour into molds. This is only for 4 popsicles.

Explosive Cheesecake

Ingredients:
- 2 8 oz. cream cheese packages (low fat or sugar free)
- 16 T Splenda
- ¼ tsp almond extract
- 3 eggs
- 1 C low fat sour cream
- 3 T Splenda
- 1 tsp vanilla extract

Directions:

1. Mix the cream cheese, sugar/Splenda, and almond extract and add the eggs one at a time.
2. Blend or whisking well, mix well and pour into deep pie pan.
3. Cook in the microwave for 20 minutes or so and turn every few minutes.
4. Store in the fridge.

Key Lime pie

Ingredients:
- 1 package unflavored gelatin
- ¼ C water
- ½ C Splenda
- ¼ tsp salt
- ½ C key lime juice
- 4 egg yolks
- 1 tsp. lime peel (grated)
- 1 container sugar free cool whip container

Directions:

1. For the crust you can get a premade pie crust from the cooler department at your grocery store.
2. Dissolve the gelatin in the water, and measure ½ C sugar and salt in saucepan and add egg whites and cream of tartar until stiff, slowly add in the sugar substitute and keep mixing.
3. Spread the meringue along the bottom of the pie crust.
4. Add grated or shaved lime peel over the cool whip.

Crème

Ingredients:
- 5 egg yolks
- 1 whole egg
- 1 qt. evaporated milk
- 1 C sugar substitute
- 2 T vanilla extract

Directions:

1. Combine the eggs and sugar in one bowl and saucepan simmer the evaporated milk then add milk to egg mixture.
2. Add ½ of the vanilla extract and stir into mixture and add pour into 8 small bowls or serving cups.
3. Cover and bake for about an hour at 350 degrees.
4. Let them cool overnight in fridge.

Chopped Strawberries

Ingredients:
- 2 1 oz. chocolate bars (semi-sweet)
- ½ T whipping cream
- 1 tsp almond extract
- ½ dozen strawberries

Directions:

1. Mix the chocolate and the whipping cream together in a glass mixing bowl and melt the chocolate in the microwave.
2. Stir in the almond extract and dip the strawberries in and set in wax paper and let them set in fridge or freezer for 15-20 minutes.

Cinnamon Crème

Ingredients:
- 1 C ricotta cheese
- 1 tsp vanilla extract
- 2 tsp cinnamon
- 2 T Splenda

Directions:
1. Mix everything together and let cool in fridge for several hours

Winter Snow pudding

Ingredients:
- 1 T gelatin
- ¼ C water
- 1 C artificial sweetener
- ¼ C lemon juice
- 3 egg whites

Directions:

1. Mix the gelatin and water and let sit to thicken up, than you can add boiling water and stir until gelatin dissolves.
2. Add the other two ingredients an place uncovered in fridge and stir ever 15-20 minutes or so.
3. Later come back and stir or mix well, add egg whites and beat softly.
4. Serve with custard sauce.

Spice Cookies

Ingredients:
- 2 C almond flour
- 1 ½ T apple spice
- ½ tsp salt
- ½ C sugar (sweetener or artificial sugar)
- 1 large egg
- ½ tsp vanilla
- 1 pack minced pecans

Directions:

1. Add everything together and bet well, form cookie dough and preheat oven to 350 degrees.
2. Bake for 12-14 minutes. Remove and let cool.

Apple Almonds

Ingredients:
- 2/3 C diced apples
- Sugar substitute
- ½ tsp cinnamon
- 3 T almond meal
- 1 tsp. butter
- 2 T chopped pecans

Directions:

1. Add the apples, cinnamon and sugar free syrup over apples and microwave for 1 ½ minutes.
2. Remove and add almond meal over the top and pecans and microwave another 1-2 minutes and serve warm.

Chocolate cookies

Ingredients:
- 2 dozen diced pecans
- 1 egg
- 1 tsp cinnamon
- 2 tsp cocoa powder
- ½ tsp vanilla extract
- 2 tsp. sugar substitute
- PAM

Directions:

1. Set oven to 350 degrees and mix all ingredients and stir cookie dough well enough to thicken it up and create small dough balls.
2. Line on baking sheet and cook for 8-10 minutes, remove and let cool before serving.

Peanut butter drops

Ingredients:
- 1 C peanut butter
- 1 C Splenda
- 1 egg

Directions:

1. Three ingredient cookies. Line baking sheet with parchment paper, and preheat oven to 350 degrees.
2. Mix ingredients, and spoon small cookie dough balls onto cookie sheet, and bake for around 10 minutes, remove and let cool.

PB&J Cookie

Ingredients:
- ¾ C Splenda
- 1 Egg
- 1 tsp vanilla extract
- 1 C peanut butter
- 1 tsp baking soda
- ¼ C sugar free grape or strawberry jelly

Directions:

1. Mix first 5 ingredients, and make small cookie dough balls and spoon onto parchment paper or greased cookie sheet.
2. Push thumb print into middle of each cookie ball for jelly after baking. Bake at 350 for 10-12 minutes.
3. After, remove from oven and let cool and spoon small spoonfuls of jelly into middle of cookies and serve.

Decadent chocolate pudding

Ingredients:
- 1C coconut milk
- ½ dozen pitted dates
- Baking cocoa

Directions:

1. You need to let the coconut sit upside down in the fridge for at least 8-10 hours.
2. You need the coconut to sink to the cream sets on the bottom. You can get rid of the milk, you just need the coconut cream part, scoop it out and add to a bowl.
3. Add the dates to the blender and a little of the coconut milk and chop or cream them in the blender. You need them as chopped/fine as possible.
4. Add the coconut cream to the blender and the 2 T baking coca and mix together.
5. Add a little more coconut milk, and add to blender until turns into creamy pudding material.

Custard

Ingredients:
- 3 eggs
- 2 ripe bananas
- 1 can coconut milk

Directions:

1. Set oven to 350 degrees, and add all of the ingredients together in the mixing bowl and blend well.
2. Take a few mason jars, and divide the ingredients into the different jars and bake for 45 minutes.

Chocolate pecan pie

Ingredients:
- 3 ½ C shredded coconut
- 5 T coconut milk
- 2 T coconut oil
- 3 ½ oz. organic chocolate bar(dark chocolate is best)
- 2 eggs
- 5 T butter
- ½ C honey
- ½ C coconut sugar
- 1 C dried shredded coconut

Directions:

1. Set the oven to 350 degrees and in a processor or blender and 2 C coconut, milk and oil and blend for around 3-4 minutes. You want this really sticky so it will hold.
2. In a separate bowl combine the coconut mixture with 1 1/3 C dried coconut and add to the pie canard spread out.
3. As for the filling, preheat your oven to 375 degrees and add the chopped up chocolate to the bottom of the crust (over the top of the coconut based crust) and in a separate bowl whisk the eggs and set aside and add melt butter, honey and palm sugar and whisk together for a few minutes and set aside to let cool.
4. Let this cool and mix in the pecans and coconut. Pour you pie filling into the crust and bake at 375 for around 20-25 minutes or until set.

Peanut Butter Cups

Ingredients:
- 4 T extra virgin coconut oil
- ½ C natural peanut butter
- ¼ C cocoa powder
- 1 ½ tsp. vanilla extract
- ½ scoop protein powder

Directions:

1. Add everything together in mixing bowl and stir together pour into cupcake tins and freeze for about 15-25 minutes or so and enjoy.

Frozen Frosting

Ingredients:
- 1-3 bananas
- Frozen berries

Directions:

1. Slice your banana into chunks and freeze for about 12-14 hours and add to a food processor along with the berries.
2. You can blend or process these until they are nice and creamy, and smooth. Like frosting or sorbet.

Brownie Balls

Ingredients:
- 2 C walnuts
- 1 C pitted dates
- 1 avocado, diced
- 2 T raw honey
- ¼ C coconut oil
- ½ tsp vanilla extract
- ½ C cocoa
- Salt to taste
- Shredded coconut
- ½ C chocolate chips

Directions:

1. Process the dates for about a minute or so. You want them to stick together for the most part.
2. Add the rest of the ingredients (minus last 2 ingredients) use that dough to make small balls then roll in the toppings and set in fridge to harden.

Peanut butter fruit dip

Ingredients:
- ½ T maple syrup
- 1 T all natural peanut butter
- 1/8 tsp cinnamon
- 6 oz. nonfat Greek yogurt

Directions:

1. Mix everything together and keep cold. Serve with apple slices or other fruits

Chai Pudding

Ingredients:
- 2/3 C cocoa powder
- 2 C almond milk
- 1 1/4 C coconut milk (nonfat)
- 1 can coconut milk (separate from other one)
- 2/3 C pure maple syrup
- 1 C dark chocolate chips
- ½ tsp salt
- 1 tsp pure vanilla extract
- 1 C chai seeds
- 1 C coconut flakes
- 1 C chopped pecans
- 1 tsp mocha coffee grinds

Directions:

1. In saucepan add coconut milk, almond milk, cocoa powder and heat in a skillet on medium heat.
2. Whisk together until smooth, and it will take a little extra work, this is really thick.
3. Remove from the heat and add rest of the ingredients, stir well and pour into container seal for at least 6 hours in the fridge.
4. After 6-8 hours serve with the chopped nuts, chocolate chips, coconut and any other topping you may want to add.

Mini cheesecakes

Ingredients:
- 2 8 oz. packets of cream cheese
- 1 C Splenda
- 2 eggs
- 1 T vanilla extract

Directions:

1. Whip everything together and pour into muffin tin cups or similar size baking cups and top with sugar free fruit jam of your choice and bake for 30 minutes or so at 350 degrees.

Apple Crisp

Ingredients:
- Cooking spray
- ¼ C sugar
- ¼ C dried cherries
- ½ C oats
- ½ C vegetable oil
- ½ C whole wheat flour
- ¼ C raw sugar
- 2 T ground cinnamon
- 9 apples, peeled and sliced
- 1 T lemon juice

Directions:

1. You can go ahead and make your crisp ahead of tie. Heat in the oven at 325 degrees, before you serve.
2. Now set your oven to 350 degrees and coat your baking dish with the cooking spray.
3. Add cherries and water in a bowl and let them soak.
4. In separate bowl add oats, oil, flour and sugar and 1 T cinnamon in a bowl and stir until well blended.
5. Add the apples to your baking dish, add water and cherries and toss lightly.
6. Sprinkle with oat toppings and bake for 40 minutes and serve warm, great with sugar free vanilla ice-cream.

South Beach Bars

Ingredients:
- 15 oz. pure pumpkin
- 12 oz. can evap. Milk (fat free)
- ½ C Egg beaters
- ¾ C Splenda
- 2 tsp. pumpkin pie spice

Directions:

1. Set your oven to 350 degrees, and add all ingredients in bowl and stir well, add the mixture to a baking dish which does need to be sprayed, then you can bake for 45 minutes or so in the oven, remove and let cool. This serves 9.

Pink Pie

Ingredients:
- 32 oz. yogurt
- 1 package sugar free strawberry or raspberry Jell-O

Directions: Mix together and let sit in fridge to harden and set. Serve with sugar free cool whip

Sour Cream cheesecake

Ingredients:
- 1 lbs. low fat cream cheese
- 16 t Splenda
- ¼ tsp. almond extract
- 3 eggs

Topping:
- 1 C fat free sour cream
- 3 packets cream cheese
- 1 tsp. vanilla extract

Directions:
1. Set your oven to 300 degrees, and fill a baking tray with water and add that to the oven, while preparing the rest.
2. Wrap foil around a baking dish. Beat the cream cheese, sugar substitute and almond extract, until light and fluffy.
3. Pour the mixture into the baking dish, and bake for one hour and twenty minutes.
4. Remove and let cool completely. Whisk topping ingredients, and add to top of cake when TOTALLY cool.

Sugar Free layered cream cheese

Ingredients:
- ½ C pumpkin puree
- 2 eggs
- ½ tsp pumpkin spice
- ½ tsp ground cinnamon
- ¼ C stevia
- ¼ raw sugar
- 2 tsp. vanilla extract
- 1 container sugar free whipped cream
- 1 graham cracker pie crust
- 2 packages light cream cheese

Directions:

1. You will add everything to the graham cracker pie crust, start with a bowl mixing with soft cream cheese and the sweetener of your choice, and your vanilla.
2. Beat until smooth and add eggs one at a time. Scoop one C aside and pour it into the crust, then add remaining ingredients and stir well, then pour over first up you added.
3. Bake for about 45 minutes. Make sure this cools before serving.
4. Often times its best to let this sit overnight.

Made in the USA
Middletown, DE
18 August 2015